Packets of Seeds

Also by H.T.A.Heisler

doctor ken
*a true story about a man
and the
Hippocratic Oath*

Coming soon:

The Innkeeper's Daughter
A Christmas story for children
with a
Christmas Carol Music Score

website: **www.DaisyHarrietteHeisler.com**

Kehnroth Schramm, M.D.
November 21, 1932 – September 24, 2004

Packets of Seeds

Words and Title by
Kehnroth Schramm, M.D., Great Spirit

describing Life after his passing
and other stories
Compiled and Edited by H.T.A. Heisler

Previous copyright printing 2007 limited edition

Author and Editor of Doctor Kehnroth Schramm's notebooks: H.T.A. Heisler

Cover design and artwork: H.T.A. Heisler

ISBN 978-0-9917756-4-4 printed book
ISBN 978-0-9917756-1-3 ebook

BISAC Spiritual/Non-fiction/Medical

Dedicated to Doctor Kehnroth Schramm's
children, grandchildren, great-grandchildren
and
all people who want to know

Table of Contents

Prologue

"I resolved never to make money at the expense of another person's suffering. For me Doctor means Teacher, not businessman. I was called to heal and be healed by words, not by money."
Kehnroth Schramm, M.D.

No truer words were ever said. Ken lived those words. He was a true physician, always wanting to be available to those in need and he wanted nothing to do with money except to use it to help those in need.

Kehnroth Schramm was a Family Physician, Psychiatrist, Teacher, Father, Grandfather, Great Grandfather, Fire keeper, and Husband.

Ken was always in search of better ways to do medicine, embracing holistic and integrative medicine long before allopathic physicians in North America accepted it. In that way Ken was a free thinker and would not change his ethics of medicine for self-preservation or for money. He lived his life protecting his Hippocratic Oath to do no harm and to protect his patients' secrets. That ran him into serious trouble.

Ken's full story is written in the book, ***doctor ken*** – a true story about a man and the Hippocratic Oath.

Ken literally gave everything away to whoever was in need as fast as it came to him; that was everything and especially knowledge to anyone who wanted it.

He did his best to feed the hungry, clothe the poor, heal the sick, heal emotional hurts, and share knowledge.

Ken would provide food, vitamins,, medicine or whatever was needed to the poor. He took care of street people regularly by providing food, clothing, accommodation on cold nights, and was known to give the coat off his back in wet and cold weather. He would stop whatever he was doing to speak with the people about their lives and to be helpful.

Everything he did was humbly. Ken never needed applause; he worked quietly. His greatest satisfaction was to bring comfort to someone and to see a child do well.

Whenever possible, Ken would share food with family and with his patients. He treasured conversation. He lived frugally, keeping only absolute essentials for himself, other than the books that he loved and read to learn what others had known. He was always researching in libraries and bookstores, and sharing his findings with whoever needed something or just wanting to share his findings out of sheer delight.

Ken gave of his time. For many years Ken volunteered long hours of work on committees about health, housing, and environmental issues, because he wanted to make a better, safer world for all people, animals and living things.

The aboriginal people of the House of Learning at the University of British Columbia draped a Pendleton Indian Friendship blanket over Ken's shoulders; the blanket had a fitting name, 'Great Spirit Robe'.

Ken has proven that life continues. He passed away September 24, 2004 but has given us the gift of his latest findings – that life does continue. He has given us this little book, *Packets of Seeds*, named by him. Also, he has proven he continues to be a physician. A story in this book called *The Healing* is a true story that happened on the first anniversary of Ken passing. The person, who had a near death experience and was expected to die, identified Ken as the spirit healer.

Easter morning, March 31, 2013, Ken surprised me with the following words:

"Everlasting life is true."

(Daisy) Harriette T.A. Heisler

"I resolved never to make money at the expense of another person's suffering. For me, Doctor means Teacher, not Businessman. I was called to heal and be healed by words, not by money."
Kehnroth Schramm, M.D.

Packets of Seeds

In the Words of

Kehnroth Schramm in Spirit

Transcribed as he told it to me after his passing.
Ken named these passages "Packets of Seeds".

Doctor Schramm was a physician and teacher. Ken crossed over September 24, 2004 and has been describing his experience of crossing over. Ken has offered these words for those of us who wonder and want to know, and for the many suffering loss and grief over a loved one. He continues to be a teacher and physician caring for us, and letting us know what is important in our lives.

Ken first gave me this poem.

my poem
now another poem
from Ken

footsteps   reunion
he led the way through the forest
rejoicing welcome join
satisfying wish to rejoin
all loneliness is gone in that moment
golden palace materialized here tonight

Then Ken requested the return of his over seventy library books. When the books were returned, these messages began.

I am light, love, young, healthy, and happy.
There is life beyond this life – a larger life.
I am very much alive.
Who would have guessed!

What holds us together is love.
We are made of light.
I am points of light in eternal bliss.

I crossed the room and comforted you [Daisy].

Meditate and I will teach you.
Meditate daily, and I will teach you.

Don't grieve for me. I am healthy and happy.
I am extremely large.
My mind and far reaching memories are intact and live on.

What keeps us together is love.
Love is unconditional on the other side.

All Ken asks for now from us, is:
"unconditional love"

I am invisible.
I see your face.
I look into your eyes.

There is no money here!
I do not need to sleep.
I do not need to eat food.

I know I am dead, but
I am acutely aware and very alive.

I will be with you instantly.

Relationships do survive death.
It is a falsehood that death ends relationships.

On being born and dying...
There is a time for everything.

It is true that words are in the universe forever.
Thoughts are deeds.
There is no secret life, all is known.

Where do you think God is?
Live life now.
Enjoy the flowers. Flowers are God's gift.
Play and listen to music, sing and dance.

Large or small... Size does not matter.
We are one with God.

Grief is a hurdle but can be conquered by
learning to live with it and replacing it with
unconditional love.

Guilt is a giant hurdle.
Let us bury the old hatchet
and just love unconditionally.

Everything is balanced.
Karma does play a role in relationships.

Ken has maintained his sense of humor, and sees and hears what is going on. He holds conversations with me about absolutely everything. Mine is the mind that wonders, and then he tells me, *"You are not present."* He comments with precision on things I do. Conversations can be very normal and even sometimes funny as he was in this life.

In answer to my questions about what it is like where he lives, Ken says he is:
"healthy, young, happy -- also in pleasure"

He tells me a bit about his being and his environment but says it is beyond my/our comprehension at this time. Explaining in detail is not really possible. What he does say is that it is: *"Peace, Love, Sincerity"*.

To understand, he says we should:
"meditate daily"

Ken has been teaching me about transfer of thought that takes place between all living things, including transfer of thought between humans and spirit, not just human to human.

Ken answers thoughts that are thought patterns a layer beneath the surface thoughts, in the subconscious. I recognize them when brought to my attention. Nothing is hidden.

In answer to a question of a concerned doubter about why he does not go somewhere where dead people go, wherever that is, Ken gave this message on May of 2007:

"I do belong on a higher plane. It would be selfish of me to stay there when so many living on earth need my help."

Friday morning, May 9th, 2007, I received a message from Ken as follows:

"Let me tell you about my crossing over…
Large doors opened.
My soul and mind entered.
I maintained memory of myself and my life.
I experienced immediate peace.
Dead friends greeted me.
We had conversation.
I see God in progress.
Realizing the Essence of Creation is light.

*Sincere prayer arranges light atoms of the
Universe, changing Time and Space.*
*Essence of all objects is swirling, throbbing
streams of light energy."*

"I have spoken."

In answer to my question regarding feelings,
how does he feel if he is light? He tells me,
"I am complete. A soul is a body."

When asked again what it is like to die, Ken
responded,
*"Think of it this way. It is like when you wake
up from a sleep, get out of bed and go for a walk
in the early morning sunshine where the air is
fresh and clean. You are awake!"*

Packets of Seeds Volume 2

Ken's advice to me: *"Be careful of delicate perception."*

In answer to my questions about what Ken is doing in spirit, he says:
I am training disciples – students.
Discourses are mental.
Disciple is a term broadly used.

I greet souls arriving – unconditional – innocent -- consciousness – permanent

I attend meetings on WISDOM.
Meetings are enjoyable beyond imagination.
Curiosity about wisdom.

I love thinking thanks.
I love thinking.

I needed to relearn the ancient language.

All thoughts vibrate eternally.
Tune out undesirable ones.
Thoughts are like a radio broadcasting,
sending and receiving.
I hear a whisper.

Whatever you believe strongly is a force.

Invisible is the difference in reality of
Time and Space.

Power is in meditation.
The centre of forehead is where single eyes
become one.

Ken brought his mother in spirit to see me; I turned away believing he was busy and I was the intruder. He then told me that he had brought her to see me because she now understands our relationship.

One day Ken told me:
"Now Earthly Karma finished. Out of the realm of karmic cosmic currents of earthly life – I have made my final exit."

Questions I ask: Why can we talk and feel each other? And how do I know it is you? Ken answered:
"Focus... Magnetism... Tied Together.
The feel is a recognition."

April 26, 2008: I am looking at the extensive library of books that Ken and I have put together on many subjects.
Ken says, *"Twenty-six letters."*

With those words comes the astonishing realization that all the ideas and stories in English books in all the libraries and bookstores are composed variations of only twenty-six letters. I have written the book *doctor ken* with only 26 letters.

April 27, 2008: I ask the questions, "What good are books? What good are my writings? Why would I write a book?"

Ken's answer: *"Teach – You/We have a responsibility to teach. People try to fit it all into the known, the expected. Like a child holding a lamp, a beacon of light open to new ways of seeing, knowing... Expect the unexpected."*

May 2009 – Ken tells me, *"Enhance the little book."* [Packets of Seeds, volume one with volume 2]

There was criticism from my relatives.
Too heavy.
My heart was too heavy over my family war.
Let us bury the old now.
You [Daisy] you, you, bury the old hatchet.

I did not want to leave in death – attached by affection to family.
I walked the next morning to assimilate my predicament of my youth – being young again.
You [Daisy] love me.
I was very sick. I am healed.
I observed God's universe.
I rushed to send telegrams – messages. I listened, listened, and listened. You [Daisy] heard.

A note from me, the writer: For twenty-four years I tried to protect Ken... I have buried his body. No one can bury his soul.

Ken has gone on to be a healer and teacher in another realm. He is light and love, young and healthy – complete. He is keeping his promise to me to let me know he is alive and he takes me to realms beyond description. Our relationship continues with a promise of eternal union. Our memory of each other continues.

Our thoughts live, affecting each other across the thin veil of a changing frequency.

As the writing of the book ***doctor ken*** took shape, it became necessary to tell the *real* story and not lose half of the true story that we experienced in the medical practice. That includes the realm of experiences beyond life and death and our physical bodies that we all, whether we are aware or not, live with. It would only be half a story to leave out what we really shared of a larger life.

I know each person is and has a multifaceted story. Ken taught me that Truth is in the beholder. This story is my/our truth.

Ken does continue to teach and with his continuing communication, he is teaching that there is an eternal life and that souls retain memory of the life they lived on earth, and that departed souls do see and hear us as we continue our sojourns on earth.

The joke is on me because in my arrogance I once said to Ken, "No living person can be my spiritual teacher." I learn that Ken is my teacher, and he does live!

My thoughts are, "I miss you, Ken."

I feel Ken's familiar touch on my head infusing me with light and fire of eternal bliss. He answers,

"I am not missing. I am with you always."

Update September 23, 2011: The writing of the book about Ken's life is finished. It is Friday morning. I am not quite awake. My brain feels like it is taking a break from remembering or even thinking. Out of the blue, Ken reminds me of the Friday morning of September 24, 2004 (the morning he passed away). Knowing that eventually I would wake up fully and remember, Ken offers a comforting reminder:

"I arrived in the morning to the irrevocable divine peace of another world healing my heart. All fear was gone."

Morning of Saturday, September 24, 2011, I ask, "How are you?"

Ken responds,

"I am great. I teach Wisdom. I know Wisdom. I teach without requiring assistance."

This comment is an inside joke that is understood between Ken and myself because I had assisted him in his medical practice and as his companion for twenty-four years, always wanting to protect him even when he insisted he did not need protection. Now he wants me to know he no longer needs protection – he is safe.

There can be no mistaken identity. These comments are so like Ken. He often says things in a way understood only between us.

November 21, 2011 — Today would be Kehnroth Schramm's birthday. His message:
"Wrote Booklet – drew in world.
Write more. I am willing. Write essay."

"Final pass. You [Daisy] have been assigned textbooks. Dear, do not worry about your life."

(My mind started to wonder, thinking about this last statement.)

Ken said, *"Thoughts are tuning out."*

This brought me back.

"Much work to do yet. You and I are blazing together in educational work."

Then in a message for the world, Ken said:

"Discard discrimination and prejudices of people of foreign lands.

Discard discrimination of differences of skin color, sex, size, age, or religion.

The goal is absolute unity – Brotherhood of humanity.

No one religion or group of people own God or have exclusive right to the 'hereafter'."

Ken has requested that I remember him as a young man.

I have been remembering him mostly as an elderly man. It comforted me to remember this time because of the unconditional love he always had for everyone, but to be honest, my selfish reasoning was that during the last two years, we were no longer working and I had him all to myself as I nursed him.

One day, when as usual, I was looking at his picture and admiring his white hair and angelic face, completely ignoring his previous descriptions of being young, he said to me, *"Stretch your mind. I am young now."*

... Love is never finished ...

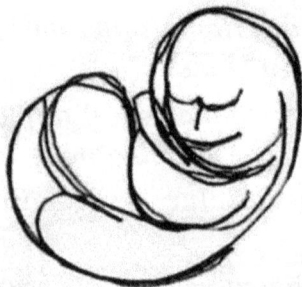

Ken (in Spirit) then gave us this one stroke image drawn very fast.

The Rose

Every now and then, people may wonder who I am talking with when I believe I am talking with Ken and receiving messages from him. One day, when I questioned, I was told I would be given a sign. In my busyness I almost forgot and was not looking for a sign.

On Valentine's Day, February 14, 2012, I bought a long stemmed red rose at a chain grocery store – no special place. On buying it, I asked for one of those small plastic tubes they put on the end of the stem with a tiny bit of water. It was late afternoon, so I drove straight to the cemetery. In other words, I did nothing to properly prepare the stem or the rose. It was just as is.

I placed the rose on Ken's grave, across Ken's chest (symbolically) where he had held his white feather. I thought it would be protective of Ken.

I asked Ken several times if he knew of the Valentine rose and got no answer.

In North Vancouver, British Columbia, Canada, we have had unusually turbulent weather since Valentine's Day. It has been up and down the temperature gauge – above and below freezing. It has been stormy with almost continuous heavy rain and several windstorms that blew furniture and other heavy items around, and downed branches of trees. It has snowed more than once.

As the stormy days came and went, the **ninth day** arrived and the rose was still in pristine shape, looking like the day I laid it over Ken, I began to take notice that something special was going on.

Saturday afternoon of **February 26**, there was a windy storm of frozen ice pellets mixed with snow that were about a half an inch in size.

Each day I have gone there expecting the rose to have blown away or succumbed to the fierce elements but it is always there just as I placed it.

It is my understanding that cut red roses should be expected to only last three to seven days with optimum care and environment.

February 28, fifteen days later – Our granddaughter Maria had come on this day to see the phenomenon of the rose. The rose was still as fresh as the day I laid it there for Ken, just opened a tiny bit more.

Last September 3rd, Maria had married. In memory of her grandfather Ken, Maria had chosen to decorate her wedding with bouquets of red roses at the ceremony and on all the banquet tables. She carried red roses in her own bouquet and she had attached Ken's lapel pin to her formal wedding gown so that Ken would be with her as she walked down the aisle to marry Luke.

On the day following the wedding, Maria laid a red rose bouquet from her wedding on Ken's grave.

Amazed on this February day, Maria took pictures of the Valentine rose on her cell phone camera, which is all we had with us. We had a break between rains and the light was low and dull in late afternoon, but the pictures came out fine.

March 2: I went there today. It is still raining after a layer of snow that hung around for about twenty-four hours and is now melted, except in some protected spots. The rose is still there and is still beautiful and strong.

March 5: It has been 21 full days. It has been pouring rain for days but today the sun came out. There are high winds blowing tree branches down again. The rose is still perfect and beautifully fresh. I picked up the rose for a minute to smell it and feel its strength – it is strong.

March 6: 22 days. I visited the rose today in sunshine and calm. The rose is still very alive and strong. Although it is the first day that there are tiny dots on the tips of some petals, a sign of getting old. It smells like a rose. Oddly, the original water in the little plastic vial on the end of the stem is as it was the day I laid the rose over Ken. The rose seems not to have needed any nourishment through the stem. It obviously has lived for over three weeks, and stayed untouched by extreme weather, on some other kind of nourishment and protection.

Ken has often said to me, *"Flowers for you."* They were thought flowers. I believe that Ken has just given me a rose – real in our dimension. I believe he has told me that he did notice the Valentine rose. I know I have been given the promised sign.

A Child's Version of Life After Life

A message from my mother came through my three-year old granddaughter who had recently been to Regina to visit with her great-grandfather.

During the night in her grandfather's home, her great grandmother appeared to the child and talked to her. Katie reported the visit happily the next morning as though it was the most natural visit. A photo album was brought out. She identified her great grandmother by picking out her picture among many. Katie was born ten months after her great-grandmother's passing and Katie had never seen a picture of her.

In the photo on the next page, Katie was drawing at my kitchen table with other children. She worked quietly and intently, producing several drawings. On that same day, she drew the picture shown here on the following page and handed it to me. She said, "Gramma, this is a message for you from your mother."

Of course, I was completely surprised.

She described the picture she had just drawn: I am standing by a body of water, crying with big tears running down; a reflection of my face is seen in the water; my mother is in the air overhead; the letters surrounding my mother is her message telling me not to cry or be sad because she is ALIVE and I should look at my reflection in the water as a peaceful mirror image of life.

Unprompted, Katie then matter-of-factly told a story of grandmothers being born as babies, then becoming a mother, then being a grandmother, then dying and being born again. Katie continued drawing.

A midwives' tale is that when a baby is born with a caul (amniotic sac) over her head, the child will become a midwife. Katie had such an interest in midwifery that whenever she could, she would wear the real stethoscope and listen intently to babies. Her favorite toy at age three was a doctor's kit. As an adult, she excels in the sciences.

IRe PooL BOOeS BLOLeK
BoLLo dhd Aie
TAbbe POOLe
I Reseieel IRe PooL LKe
reLkeekor Ayohb PoeK

The Healing

A TRUE STORY

IT HAPPENED SEPTEMBER 2005, on the First Anniversary of Ken's passing. A miraculous healing happened in the Foothills Hospital in Calgary, Alberta, Canada, where Ken had been a Senior Resident Physician in the Department of Psychiatry, studying and teaching Family Psychiatry in the years of 1973 and 1974.

A young man, an insulin dependant diabetic also fighting an addiction to street drugs, alcohol, and smoking, was already in poor health when he had a truck accident that seriously damaged his hand. He required an operation to repair his hand. A hospital borne Staph infection entered the wound. He ended up in the Intensive Care Unit with MRSA (Methicillin-resistant Staphylococcus aureus) that had traveled from his hand to his lungs. He was now dying of this infection and resulting pneumonia with no available medicine. He lay unconscious for several days in ICU. The attending physicians did not expect him to live. His family arrived from another province to be with him at the end, when he suddenly woke up, hysterical.

He had tubes removed from his throat just hours before in preparation for death, so now he had difficulty speaking. "Mom, was Ken a fire keeper?" were his first words. "I think it was Ken!"

[This man lived in Alberta and though he had met Ken briefly, he had absolutely no knowledge that Ken was a fire keeper.]

He was hysterically trying to tell about his experience. "It was Ken who healed me. There were two elders accompanying Ken who looked like whites, one male and one female, but they were really native souls. Ken, the fire keeper, gave me a choice to live or die. I chose to live. So the fire keeper hung me upside down for two to four hours and kept my fire burning. I had a near death experience and a fire keeper helped me. I was given this aboriginal name so that I could have life."

He was trying so hard to say the name and make it sound the same as he knew it; his mouth was twisting and tears were falling because it was not a word from his vocabulary. He spoke, "TNE"; then suggested it might be "ENT". Quickly he resolved it was TNE, but when he spoke the word it sounded more like "T Hee N EE". He said it several times. Then he said, "I was told groups of three cling to TNE."

He told his mother that he had not realized until this experience that souls are different, opposite or upside down. He said, "Souls are fusions of light!"

Looking for answers, the mother had made notes and telephoned Daisy from the hospital. Daisy knew that two friends had died of hospital borne staph infection in a Vancouver hospital just weeks before and over the years, Daisy had known of several other deaths in Vancouver hospitals because of hospital borne infections. So, this sudden waking up was like a miracle. But answers were being sought. Daisy offered to ask Ken's friends, aboriginal elders John and N'kixw'stn.

Over night Daisy received part answer from Ken.

"The tree of life is the human body. A baby in final months of gestation is head down and feet upwards. A normal birth is head first, feet last. The young man was put upside down. I gave a cosmic current that was the fire, to rejuvenate the brain and spinal center, and get oxygen flowing."

Then an answer arrived from N'kixw'stn.

"I got a response about the TNE immediately. I have an aboriginal word in my language that means "BUTTERFLY". Just say the three letters quite fast and it sounds like "Tee-N-Eee". Bring it to my language it will sound like this: "TEE-HE-HONN-KNEE". Now what you have to do is to think about what the butterfly does. The butterfly goes from one flower to the next extracting nectar from the flower. Butterflies are also beautiful. The most amazing fact about the butterfly is it's migration pattern. That alone proves how powerful they are, but yet they are so fragile."

At sunrise Daisy emailed the answers to the mother along with an additional note:

"The native elder tells me that TEE-HE-HONN-KNEE in her language means BUTTERFLY. Butterfly means Transformation. 'Groups of three cling to TNE' are the caterpillar, the cocoon, and then transformation takes place and the butterfly flies free.

"We are the mirror image of our astral body. We are three bodies -- physical, astral, and causal.

"Ken has described himself as points of light.

"Also, Antony reminds me that in Chinese medicine, some meridians of the body run from bottom to top. The young man has had a near death experience and a rebirth. He was held upside down to receive the infusion of light. He is now in a transformation of his life."

AFTER BEING RELEASED from the hospital and free of MRSA in subsequent testing, he had been wondering why he was brought back to life... to do what great work? He traveled to visit with Daisy and posed the question. She slept on the question that night.

In the new morning, Daisy told the young man, "It is possibly very simply that one boy, your son, needs a father and that is the special work you must do. That is the answer for most parents. The job of parenting is as important as any job on earth. It is a gift."

[At this time of writing this book, seven and a half years have passed since September 2005; the young man is free of MRSA and free of drug and alcohol addictions. The young man continues life by working, heading up large projects. And he is a caring parent.]

Each of us human beings is here in this world on Planet Earth to manifest, express, be, do that unique gift/part of creation that we are. Our task is to become human beings, sharing the gifts we have been given and the gifts that we are, with all our relations, human and non-human, becoming indigenous, at home in balance with the places we inhabit and co-create, in the process of living and dying.

Kehnroth Schramm, M.D.

Finis
Love is never finished...

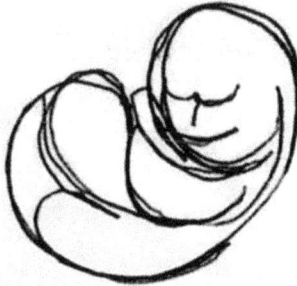

Kehnroth Schramm, M.D. 1932-2004

doctor ken at Kitsilano Beach circa 1990
Vancouver, British Columbia
Canada

www.ingramcontent.com/pod-product-compliance
Lightning Source LLC
Chambersburg PA
CBHW030311030426
42337CB00012B/674